LIFE-SIZE
DRAGONS

WRITTEN BY
JOHN GRANT

ILLUSTRATED BY
FRED GAMBINO

Sterling Publishing Co., Inc.
New York

Library of Congress Cataloging-in-Publication Data Available

10 9 8 7 6 5 4 3

Published in 2006 by Sterling Publishing Co., Inc.
387 Park Avenue South, New York, NY 10016

First published in the UK in 2006 by Chrysalis Children's Books,
An imprint of Chrysalis Books Group plc
The Chrysalis Building, Bramley Road, London W10 6SP
Text © 2006 by John Grant
Illustrations © 2006 by Fred Gambino
Concept © 2004 by David Bergen

Distributed in Canada by Sterling Publishing
c/o Canadian Manda Group, 165 Dufferin Street
Toronto, Ontario, Canada M6K 3H6

Color Reproduction by Dot Gradations Ltd UK
Printed in China

Sterling ISBN-13: 978-1-4027-2536-4
            ISBN-10: 1-4027-2536-1

For information about custom editions, special sales, premium and
corporate purchases, please contact Sterling Special Sales
Department at 800-805-5489 or specialsales@sterlingpub.com.

A note about scientific names
The scientific (taxonomic) names for
Earth's plants and animals look like Latin,
and quite often they are, but many consist
of made-up or just bad Latin, sometimes
with a bit of Greek thrown in. The names
of dragon species follow the same format.

WHERE DO DRAGONS COME FROM?

Dragons are the world's most mysterious creatures. Some people think dragons are related to dinosaurs, but survived when dinosaurs died out about 65 million years ago. Others think dragons come from an unknown star system or from a parallel universe. But the truth is far stranger than that. . . .

We are not alone

On the far side of the Sun, where we can never see it, is another world exactly like Earth. The ancient Greeks called this planet Antichthon. (*Anti* means "opposite," *chthon* means "Earth." The *ch* is pronounced like a "k.")

On Earth, the dinosaurs were wiped out by a catastrophe about 65 million years ago. Antichthon suffered no such disaster, so its dinosaurs survived a while longer. The reptiles that had wings became the most important animals on Antichthon, especially after they developed an astonishing new ability – they could breathe fire.

Dragons originate from Antichthon, a planet that has continents like our continents, and seas and clouds and skies like ours.

Accidental visitors

Because Earth and Antichthon are so like each other, sometimes there is a slight overlap between the two worlds. Events that should have happened in one world happen in the other. Dragons belong to Antichthon, not to Earth. But sometimes a dragon can accidentally stray into our world. Most often, these accidental visits go unnoticed, because they do not last very long. Sometimes, though, a dragon is unable to find its way home to its own world. The result can be chaos! Dragons are dangerous, especially when threatened.

Dinosaurs and dragons

Until about 65 million years ago, Earth and Antichthon had very similar stories. Both worlds were dominated by all the different species (types) of dinosaurs. On Antichthon, however, the dinosaurs ruled the world somewhat longer, until about 40 million years ago.

Some dinosaurs had large plates and fins on their backs. These were probably used as a type of protection or to help the large reptiles lose heat. Some of these dinosaurs began to glide using the front two of their plates, and eventually these two plates became wings that could flap up and down.

Over time, some types of winged dinosaurs – the first dragons! – began to breathe fire. We do not know precisely how this ability developed, or how soon it came along after the first dragons had taken to the air. But breathing fire was a tremendous advantage. Although some dinosaurs still exist on Antichthon, most were wiped out by their descendants, the dragons.

LIFE-SIZE

Life-size stamp

This stamp shows which illustrations are drawn life-size. When a dragon is shown on a smaller scale, the symbol of a horse or an adult human hand is sometimes shown to give a sense of how large the dragon is.

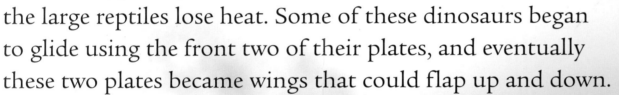

Fire fight

Early dragons had to compete with dinosaurs. For millions of years, the two groups battled for survival. Eventually the dragons triumphed – because they could fly, and because they could breathe fire. Scenes like this must once have been common on Antichthon. The *Tyrannosaurus rex* is bigger and more powerful, but the dragon can fly and dodge its claws. And the *T. rex* has no defense against the dragon's lethal bursts of flame.

Contents

Early dragons

Some of the early dragons looked a bit like the ancestors of the birds on Earth. They were about the same size, too – *Draco escalensis*, for example, was the size of a large turkey. As time went on, bigger and bigger dragons evolved. The monster *Draco rex* still roams Antichthon's skies today. *Varanus sinensis*, a modern species known as the Oriental or Chinese dragon, however, is slightly smaller than *Draco escalensis*. But what it lacks in size, it makes up for in intelligence.

Draco escalensis

LIFE-SIZE

The early dragon Draco escalensis *had a beak, and overall, its head reminds us of a chicken's or a turkey's. Although* Draco escalensis *was relatively small, the beak must have been a fearsome weapon for this predatory carnivore.*

ANATOMY OF A DRAGON

The biggest dragons are the biggest flying animals Antichthon has ever known, and they are far bigger than any flying creature there has ever been on Earth. Because they can fly, because they are quick-moving and incredibly strong, because they can breathe fire, because of their big, sharp teeth and their claws, dragons can be truly terrifying! It comes as a surprise that even the most ferocious don't kill for meat all that often. Mostly they eat plants. Dragons need plenty of plants in their diet if they are to breathe fire.

How dragons are born

Baby dragons hatch from eggs. The mother can lay eggs as often as once every few weeks, but the bigger dragon species lay eggs only once or twice a year. Usually the mother lays six to ten eggs at once, but some desert species of dragons may lay 100 or more.

Draco rex females lay six to eight eggs. These take about seven months to hatch. The babies chew and claw their way out of the shells. For the first few hours afterward, they are very vulnerable. Their claws are not fully hard, they cannot breathe fire, and their eyes cannot focus properly yet. If their mother did not look after them, they would be easy prey. She feeds them, and soon they can breathe small flames.

LIFE-SIZE

Tails and scales

The body and wings of dragons like *Draco rex* and *Draco extravagans* are covered in red or orange lozenge-shaped scales. The scales are made of a tough substance called *chitin*. It is the same stuff that crab shells are made of. But dragon scales are much thicker than a crab shell, and they overlap to give the dragon's body even better protection. Only on the tummy and neck are they a bit thinner.

The scales extend right down onto the dragon's tail, which is a powerful weapon in the dragon's armory. The dragon can use its tail like a club to pulverize enemies, or can lash it like a whip to deliver disabling or fatal blows.

The lethality of the tail as a weapon is enhanced by the upright plates along its length and in particular by the tip. This is like a barbed arrowhead, and can be driven into the enemy with devastating force.

Barbed tail of Draco extravagans

Draco minoris *and* Draco gambini *are far smaller than their cousin* Draco rex, *but you still wouldn't want to pick a fight with either of them! Their wings and feet are lethally clawed.*

Clawed feet

If the claws on the wings are fearsome, the talons on the feet are even worse! Most dragons have four "toes," each with a sharp claw. On *Draco rex*, these claws grow even longer than the wing claws, and they're much thicker and tougher. There's another claw at the back of the heel. The claws at the front are for gripping and slashing. The claw at the back is for deep gouging.

LIFE-SIZE

Foot of Draco gambini

Wing of Draco minoris

Learning to fly

As soon as baby *Draco rex* dragons can see clearly, their parents teach them to fly. The father takes one at a time in his claws and flies high into the air. Then he just drops the baby! Most baby dragons get the idea fast and are flying by the time they reach their mother, waiting far below. A few don't, and if they're lucky, she catches them so they can try again. Sadly, some are snatched out of the air by predators – often primitive wild dragons.

Clawed wings

Early dragons had wings like a bat's. They were easily damaged. A dragon with a damaged wing can't fly and is very soon a dead dragon. But the wings of dragons slowly evolved to be more powerful, with tough scales like those covering the rest of the dragon's body.

A dragon's wing has three joints. One is at the shoulder, where the wing joins the body. You could think of the other two as being like our elbow and wrist. Early dragons had a bony knob at the "wrist" joint. As dragons evolved, the knob became bigger and sharper. Species like *Draco minoris* and *Draco rex* have a hard, sharp curved claw where the bony knob used to be.

How many heads?

Most species of dragon have just one head. But, over
millions of years, some species evolved to have extra heads.
A few of the dragons that have strayed to Earth have had *lots*
of heads. It seems many-headed dragons have died out on
Antichthon – certainly none have strayed to Earth
for thousands of years. It is hard to know why
many-headed dragons evolved at all.

*Like its single-
headed counterparts,
Draco triceps had
deceptively dainty forefeet,
or "hands." All dragons use their
"hands" and sharp-clawed "fingers"
to perform delicate tasks, just as we
do – or to shred the flesh of enemies.*

Draco triceps

The eyes of a dragon are very sensitive to the slightest motion. The dragon is, however, disadvantaged by the fact that its eyes are at the sides of its head, not the front, like ours. This means it does not have good stereoscopic vision – that is, it cannot easily judge how close things are.

When you first look at a dragon's head, you might think there are no ears at all. Not so! Dragon ears do not have external flaps, like ours, but are buried beneath a thin, scaly layer, which is usually circular or oval and sits behind the eyes.

A dragon's hearing is far less acute than ours: if you stood near a dragon and whispered, the dragon probably could not hear you. The dragon ear cannot detect the higher sounds we can hear. However, it is sensitive to some sounds that are too low for us to hear.

A dragon's nostrils play a part in the breathing of fire, but they are also, like ours, involved in the sense of smell. It is believed dragons can actually smell gold and jewels, and it is likely that this is the main reason why they are so skilled at finding jewelry and precious metals.

A Greek myth?

The Hydra that Hercules fought in the ancient Greek legends was one of the many-headed species of dragon. It is hard to know how literally we can take this myth. It was probably exaggerated as people told it to each other. It is quite possible the Hydra had nine heads – dragons with that number are known to have existed – but it is unlikely that every time Hercules chopped a head off, another grew instantly in its place!

FIRE-BREATHING

Draco protuberans

The dragon is the only animal that can breathe fire. Dragons use the flames as a weapon, of course, but that's not all – there are more peaceful uses, too. Until recently, people thought fire-breathing could be done only by magic. Now we know better.

Fuel for the fire

Like any other fire, the blazing breath of a dragon needs fuel. And their fuel is . . . natural gas! The gas that dragons produce inside themselves is called methane. Methane is the main constituent of the natural gas people use for heating and cooking. This methane is formed from coal and oil. We form some methane in our digestive systems, too, but not nearly as much as dragons do. As dragons digest the plants they eat, their digestive systems produce lots of methane gas. Dragons need big bellies to create enough methane to fuel the flames, but their bellies cannot be too big as this would hinder their ability to fly.

Spa. king the infe. no

When some types of crystal are pressed hard, they generate electricity. This property is called piezoelectricity. (*Piezo* comes from an ancient Greek word meaning "to press.") Sometimes the electricity produces a spark. Adult dragons have piezoelectric crystals at the back of their throat.

Crystals of the common mineral quartz can produce a spark by piezoelectricity. As a dragon eats food, it also swallows small bits of sand and earth. Its body holds onto the quartz in the sand and this travels through the bloodstream to two glands at the rear of the throat. These glands secrete the quartz into special cavities near the back of the jaw, at the top and the bottom. There, the quartz forms into crystals. When the dragon grinds its teeth in a certain way, the crystals produce a spark, and – *bang!* – fire!

Baby dragons can't breathe fire at first, but soon start growing crystals, thanks to rock dust and sand eaten with their food.

Metallic blood

Like us, dragons need iron in their blood to carry oxygen around their bodies. But they can use other metals as well – gold, copper, silver and platinum. These metals help fire-breathing by enabling the crystals of quartz to form and also because of their electrical conductivity. Mainly, dragons get the metals from their diet, just as we get iron from ours, but they also like to suck on metallic ores and metal objects. No wonder dragons like gold coins so much!

Fiery breath

The bigger the dragon, the bigger the flame it can produce, and the largest dragons, like *Draco rex*, can blast fire as far as 330 feet (100m), sometimes farther. However, they cannot keep this up for very long as the methane in their belly runs out and they have to wait for more to be made. The smallest dragons, only a little bigger than a pigeon, produce tiny flames. Here we see the inferno raging in the jaws of a full-grown *Draco rex*.

LIFE-SIZE

Draco rex jaws

HOW CLEVER ARE DRAGONS?

We know dragons have fairly big brains, and a large brain usually means that an animal is clever. But what's important for intelligence is not just the size of the brain, but how wrinkled its surface is and how many "automatic" things it must do – like control walking and breathing. We do not know exactly how wrinkled dragon brains are, but we do know their brains must not just handle the "automatic" things our own brains do, but also control the wings and cope with all the problems of flight. We think the brightest dragons are about as intelligent as humans, whereas Chinese dragons (*Varanus sinensis*) may be far more clever than we are!

Brawn versus brains

Among early dragons, it seems the smaller ones were the clever ones. *Draco escalensis* was the size of a turkey, and *Draco extravagans* the size of a horse. They lived at the same time and are both now long extinct. Though *Draco extravagans* was much bigger, its brain was only slightly larger. It is probable that small dragons, less able to fight back against predators, had to be quick-witted to avoid trouble.

Communication

Dragons use sounds and display to communicate with each other, just as we do. *Draco faseolo* has a most unusual means of producing sounds. Like many of our own world's creatures, some dragons use sounds to attract a mate. The spines of the crests on *Draco faseolo* males produce whistling sounds when the wind blows through them, or when the dragon moves his head swiftly. These sounds would seem pretty strange to your ears – perhaps even ghastly – but to a female dragon they must be the sweetest music!

LIFE-SIZE

Draco faseolo

The most intelligent species

This is the brain of Varanus sinensis. *Like our brains, its surface is greatly wrinkled, a sign of its intelligence.*

The small dragons that stray from Antichthon into China and other parts of East Asia are of the species *Varanus sinensis* and are very different to *Draco rex* and related dragons. They have little wings, big horns on their heads, and they are far less ferocious than *Draco rex* – indeed, they are gentle and kindly. They are also very intelligent. The ancient Chinese thought dragons were so wise that they said the dragons were gods! This is why in some Chinese processions you see big dragons made of paper being carried along.

LIFE-SIZE

SURVIVAL OF THE FITTEST

Modern-day dragons are colorful and sophisticated creatures, and many are huge animals and effective predators. But the very earliest dragons were quite small and drab. Most lived in jungle undergrowth and survived by avoiding the big dinosaur meat-eaters.

The dragons' earliest ancestors

Lizards of all varieties swarmed in the undergrowth of Antichthon's jungles 150 million years ago. Among them were some that were distinguished by single or double rows of sharkfin-like plates running down their backs. These plates seem to have first developed as climbing or burrowing aids, but we are not sure. In some species, the plates near the head grew larger than the others, probably because they were useful in fights. Eventually, after tens of millions of years of competition and evolution, these bigger plates would become wings.

One of these lizards was *Varanus urdraconis*, which was most widespread about 80 million years ago. It seems to have survived largely on insects and burrowing grubs.

The plates nearest the head are beginning to look like rudimentary wings.

LIFE-SIZE

Varanus urdraconis

Mammals – rivals of the dragons

Dragons were not the only small animals that ran in fear of the dinosaurs. There were also little ratlike creatures that seem to have been relatively intelligent. On our own planet, the mammals became highly successful – they went on to inherit Earth! No one knows for sure why this did not happen on Antichthon. We can only guess there was a contest between the early dragons and the early mammals, and the dragons won. This probably came about when the dragons evolved wings. Flight was an advantage the mammals could never overcome.

Bigger, faster, brighter

By about 60 million years ago, some of the little ground lizards had evolved into something more formidable. Species like *Draco serpens* were 3.3 feet (1m) or more longer and they had prominent jaws containing razor-sharp teeth. They could raise the front of their bodies for long periods, running on their two hindlegs so their forelegs were free to manipulate objects. They could not yet fly, but the well-developed plates near their heads probably helped them adopt a sort of semi-gliding gait, enabling them to run more swiftly.

Draco serpens

This ground-based lizard already shows some of the characteristics of its future descendants – the dragons.

DRAGONS OF EXTREME CLIMATES

All the different types of dragons are superbly adapted to the way they live on Antichthon. They can be found in the hottest and coldest of climates, on land and in the sea, on mountaintops and in jungles.

Water dragons

For centuries human sailors have talked about the huge monsters they sometimes meet at sea. It seems certain these are marine dragons that have strayed into our world.

If you looked into the mouth of a *Draco marini*, the sea-dwelling dragon species, you wouldn't see teeth, but you would see what look like millions of tiny hairs. Even though sea dragons have a terrifying reputation and have been known to attack and kill whales, sharks and other big sea animals, most of the time they feed on tiny creatures called krill. The dragon sucks in water, closes its mouth, then blows out the water through its nose. The tiny krill are trapped by the "hairs."

Draco marini

Spreading their wings

About 40 million years ago, there was a sudden surge
in dragon evolution. This was linked to the ability to fly.
The ability to breathe fire probably followed soon after.
With these twin advantages over the dinosaurs, it was
not too long before the dragons took over as the
dominant type of creature on Antichthon.
Now that they were predators rather
than prey, the way was open for
evolution to experiment
with the dragons.

*About 38 million years ago,
the most magnificent dragons
started appearing. And few
have been more splendid
than Draco effulgens.*

Draco effulgens

Draco effulgens

This young Draco effulgens *dates from about ten million years ago and is already showing most of the features of modern specimens.* Draco effulgens *is probably the most resplendent animal on either of the two planets.*

Getting attention

Once they were no longer prey, the dragons could become as colorful as nature would allow, so many species became more and more spectacular. Just as peacocks and other animals on Earth use displays of bright colors to attract a mate, so do dragons. Their scales can be red, silver, gold, green, blue and other colors. Their wings and chests can show every color of the rainbow.

Their tails today are far longer than in early times, and often have vividly colored plumes. Many species also developed plumes of hair, or brightly hued spines, on their heads.

Some people believe that a monster lives in Loch Ness, a lake in Scotland. This creature is likely to be the freshwater dragon species, Draco nessii, *which must have crossed over from Antichthon and become trapped on Earth.*

Which came first?

The evolution of water-dwelling dragons presents something of a mystery. They emerged at about the same time as the flying dragons did. Were they just a different branch of the dragon family whose prominent shoulder plates became flippers rather than wings? Instead of this theory, most scientists think that they were land dragons that adapted to the water to escape the worst of the major ice age that raged on Antichthon at one time.

Dragons of the shoreline

Shoreline dragons have sleek bodies adapted for swimming, but they still look more like the dragons of land and air than like sea dragons. They have full-size wings, which they use in the same way that diving birds on Earth do. Because being able to breathe fire is not much use to them when hunting fish, they do not have nearly such big bellies as the dragons of land and air.

Draco glacialis

Jungle dragons

In thick tropical jungles and rainforests, the spreading upper branches of the trees form a canopy that can extend hundreds of miles (km) in every direction. Dragons build their nests in branches under this canopy. Adult dragons can withstand the tropical sun's heat, but their eggs are more vulnerable – the shade of the canopy stops the eggs from "cooking" before the baby dragons hatch!

The dragons spend much of their waking time flying high above the canopy, searching for food. They catch birds on the wing, or swoop to snatch mammals from the upper branches. Mostly, of course, they eat the leaves and flowers of the trees, which they need to generate methane for fire-breathing.

Draco jangalae

Dragons of the ice

Antichthon suffers ice ages like those on Earth. Ice ages usually
last many millions of years. Dragons are better able to survive
long periods of bitter cold than we are because, although the
plants and animals that they depend on become much rarer,
they can fly long distances and search vast areas to find them.
Their ability to breathe flames helps as well – they can light fires
to keep themselves warm! At the end of the last Antichthonian
Ice Age, when the glaciers retreated, some dragons had become
so good at living in icy places that they preferred to stay in them.

THE LURE OF GOLD

In all the legends about dragons, one thing stands out. Dragons are *really* fond of gold! When they find themselves on Earth, they do their best to get hold of treasure. Jewels and all kinds of treasure attract them, but it's gold they like best of all. Why do dragons like precious metals so much? It's because the quartz crystals in their jaws work best to light their fiery breath when the dragon's bloodstream contains plenty of metals. Their food contains tiny amounts of metal, but dragons also like to chew on metal objects before spitting them out, and this also allows the metals to enter their bloodstream.

Ancient gold rushes

The earliest fire-breathing dragons did not know their bodies needed gold, but they found they felt better and could spark flames more easily if they drank from some streams rather than others. And the streams they preferred ran through gold-rich areas, and so had traces of gold in the water.

Later, the most intelligent species learned to seek gold out. Early dragon settlements formed in areas where the ground contained a lot of gold. The dragons worked together to dig out the gold. So it was because of gold that the first dragon civilizations started. They began as simple settlements clustered around a gold mine.

Desert dragons

Desert dragons spend a lot of time on the surface, soaking up warmth from the Sun, but they must tunnel underground for food and water. These dragons, therefore, have streamlined bodies, almost like water dragons. They spread their wings to catch sunlight when on the surface, but fold them in tight to their body when underground. The dragons writhe through the sand like worms. They swallow the sand ahead of them, sucking plants or tiny animals out of it. They excrete the sand behind them.

Some small species of desert dragon hide themselves under the sands at the bottom of a shallow pit. Any animal that comes along and falls into the pit is . . . instant supper!

LIFE-SIZE

Underground eggs

Desert dragons lay their eggs under the sand to keep them cool. A mother desert dragon can lay over 100 eggs at once, but sometimes only a few survive. When the baby dragons hatch, they tunnel to the surface and spread their wings for the first time.

Draco aridus

Silvery scales, shimmering wings

Draco glacialis, the species that lives in Antichthon's polar regions, is among the most beautiful of all dragons. Its scales are like polished silver, and it has plumes of long, fine silver hair on its head, and when these plumes move, they look like waterfalls. The silvery scales help keep the dragon warm – shiny surfaces lose less heat than non-shiny ones.

The wings of *Draco glacialis* are important for attracting a mate. The underside of a male ice dragon's wings is truly spectacular. Think of the shimmering, glistening colors you see on the surface of an oily puddle. Those are the colors you see when a male *Draco glacialis* fully extends his wings. The underside of a female's wings is beautiful as well, but less spectacular. Here the colors are generally browns and greens – colors that offered good camouflage in the warmer climates where the ice dragons' distant ancestors lived.

The dragons of the frozen regions have extra-long talons on their feet for gripping the ice and for catching fish through holes that the dragons melt in the ice with their fiery breath. *Draco glacialis* also has long fangs with which to chip and chew deep into the ice in search of food.

Treasures

Dragons stranded in our world can hardly believe their luck. They don't have to go digging for the gold they crave – we've done that for them! And our jewelry and coins sometimes contain other metals – metals like copper, silver, and platinum. Platinum is even better than gold at helping a dragon's crystals spark fire. No wonder that, when dragons find treasure, they hoard it, guarding it fiercely against anyone else who might want it. A mound of gold coins could last a dragon for life, and leave plenty to pass on to their offspring.

Communing with the wild

Although we know next to nothing about dragons'
innermost feelings, we know they are spiritual beings.
They have no religion or other superstition, but they often
spend long periods in meditation, pondering the meaning
of their existence. Perhaps this is why they are still drawn
to the wilderness – where the quiet and splendor form
fitting backdrops to their contemplation.

The dragon world

Unlike on Earth, where human civilization is very widespread, on Antichthon the major centers of dragon civilization are confined to fairly small areas – those areas that are rich in gold. The vast majority of dragons still choose to live in Antichthon's enormous wilderness regions – and they have adapted perfectly to life in the mountains, jungles, oceans and rivers. Even the dragons that belong to large communities like to spend much of their time in remote places. It is as if dragons have not yet been entirely convinced that civilization is a good thing.

DRAGON CIVILIZATION

Over the past few thousand years, some dragon species have learned to live together and cooperate. On Earth, people learned this long ago, because of agriculture. Dragons don't need agriculture – they can fly to find food. But in communities, other things are easier, like looking after the young, old, and sick. Over time, dragon communities became centers not just of care, but of knowledge and culture.

The arts

Although dragons sometimes draw or carve symbols that other dragons can recognize, they have no writing. Nor do they have painting or sculpture. But in one art, they reign supreme: self-decoration. From early times, dragons have used display to attract mates. Their spread wings can offer a spectacular show. At some point, dragons learned to use muds and plant dyes to daub their scales and plumes with vivid patches of color. Later, they started to paint their faces and especially their claws.

LIFE-SIZE

Jewelry

Dragon communities contain craftworker dragons, especially metalworkers. Once dragons had learned about human jewelry, they discovered how to work metals. They use their fiery breath to extract metals from ores and to heat metals until they're soft and moldable. Today's dragon may have fully painted claws, a dyed plume, rings on its claws and horns, bands on its ankles, a breastplate and a crown!

A meeting of minds

In the past, dragons were largely solitary creatures, combining at most into small groups. Relatively recently, some have learned the advantages of living in communities, although they may still take months at a time away from home in search of solitude. Most recently of all, the dragons of all the communities around the world have begun to congregate once every four years. We're not quite sure what this huge meeting is about, but it must be a magnificent sight.

DRAGON SLAYERS

Throughout the history of our own world there have been legends of heroes who have fought fierce dragons and killed them. Not all dragons are dangerous, but some are. . . .

The dragon of gold

In Greek mythology, the hero Cadmus was the son of the king of Phoenicia. Two of his friends were killed by an enormous golden dragon that breathed fire. After a fierce struggle, Cadmus managed to kill the dragon. A voice told him to plant the teeth of the dragon, like seeds. He did this, and from the earth sprang an army of soldiers, one for each tooth. The soldiers took Cadmus as their leader and helped him build his great city of Thebes.

Sigurd and Fafnir

Sigurd, also known as Siegfried, was a hero in Norse and German legends. There was a dragon called Fafnir that hoarded its treasure in a cave. After Sigurd had killed Fafnir for the dragon's gold, he absentmindedly licked his fingers. He discovered he could now understand what birds were saying. The birds told him he should eat the dragon's heart because it would give him great wisdom.

Saintly dragon slayer

Saint George, visiting the city of Silene in Libya, found it being terrorized by a dragon that lived in the nearby lake. The dragon said it would destroy the city if it were not fed with the people's children, chosen by lottery each day. The day Saint George arrived, it was the turn of the king's daughter. He waited until the dragon came out of the water and fatally wounded it with his lance.

Saint George, the patron saint of England, was probably born in Turkey in the 3rd century. He was a soldier in the Roman Army when he became a Christian.

Quetzalcóatl, the dragon god

This dragon was not slain by a hero but was a hero himself! The Toltec and earlier peoples of Mexico had legends of a winged, feathered serpent called Quetzalcóatl. He was a wise leader who invented books and the calendar. At last, though, he was defeated by Tezcatlipoca, the god of the night sky, and sailed off into the east.

In the 16th century, Spanish invaders arrived in Mexico, sailing from the east. The Aztec people thought they had been sent by Quetzalcóatl, and they welcomed them as messengers from the serpent-god.

DRAGONS AND THE MODERN WORLD

We don't see dragons around much today. Fewer of them have strayed here since the end of the Middle Ages, five centuries ago. What has happened to them all? Some people think dragons have learned how to avoid being trapped on Earth. Others think dragons may be in trouble on their home world, possibly because of global warming, a huge problem on Earth. On our planet, most of the warming is caused by the gases released when things are burned. Could great forest fires ignited by the dragons' fiery breath have spurred catastrophic global warming on Antichthon?

Komodo dragon

LIFE-SIZE

Fossilized dragons?

In parts of Siberia, the bodies of mammoths are sometimes discovered in the ice. The mammoths have been so well preserved that their meat can still be fresh enough to eat. What is less well known is that mammoths are not the only ancient creatures to have been found there. No complete dragon corpses have been uncovered, but sometimes fossilized dragon bones are found. Many scientists say the fossils are not those of dragons, but of dinosaurs . . . but who can be sure?

Just like some people hunt dinosaur fossils, others hunt dragon fossils. There aren't many of these "dragon-hunters" alive today, and they tend to be secretive.

Cryptozoology

It looks like just a long, incomprehensible word, but some people take the science of cryptozoology very seriously. (*Crypto* means "hidden.") The aim of the cryptozoologist is to find living or fossil examples of animal species unknown to modern science. Many people say cryptozoologists are crazy, but every few years big animals are discovered no one knew about before. Will dragons be next?

Perhaps one day you'll be lucky enough to find the fossil of a jawbone like this. If so, you'll become very famous!

Jawbone of a young Draco rex

LIFE-SIZE

Earth's own dragons

No dragons have ever evolved on Earth. But there are some creatures *called* dragons because they look rather like real ones. They do not breathe fire and they do not fly, but they are very dangerous. They are the biggest lizards in the world. They live around the remote Komodo Island in Indonesia. Their scientific name is *Varanus komodoensis*, but most people call them giant monitors, dragon lizards, or Komodo dragons. An adult can be more than 10 feet (3m) long and weigh more than 285 pounds (130kg) – nearly twice as heavy as many adult humans. Komodo dragons can live for as long as a century.

They mostly eat dead animals. But they can kill for food as well – and they can be vicious killers. You would not want to pick a fight with one! They can run quite quickly and have big, powerful claws and lots of very sharp teeth. They have been known to kill people for food. Sometimes they kill and eat each other. Most of the few Komodo dragons that survive today live in special reserves.

INDEX

Author's confession

There is no such planet as Antichthon, although some of the ancient Greeks thought there was. And there are no such creatures as dragons, despite all the legends. Nor have dragon fossils been found. Sea serpents and lake monsters are probably just myths, or distorted accounts of something else. What I have tried to do in this book is tell you what dragons would be like if they were real.

The information about ice ages, dinosaurs, Komodo dragons and climate change is all true, and the legends are genuine legends. The Aztecs really did think the Spanish were messengers from Quetzalcóatl . . . and they suffered terribly for this mistake.